THE NZ BOOK.

Jess Lunnon
Sandi Mackechnie

Illustrators

Nigel Beckford
Michael Fitzsimons

Concepts, Art Direction, Text

THE NZ BOOK

Published 2012 by FitzBeck Publishing
www.nzbook.co.nz

Contact
Tel: 04 8019669
PO Box 10399, The Terrace, Wellington 6143

ISBN
978-0-473-20788-5

SORRY ELIZABETH

As professional writers we have travelled the length and breadth of New Zealand many times over the last 20 years – from the oyster farms of Houhura harbour in the far north, to remote East Coast marae, to Bluff's fishing fleet at the foot of the country.

We have interviewed all sorts – teachers, farmers, doctors, nurses, Ministers of the Crown, students, parents, captains of industry, workers in every industry under the sun. Sometimes we hear an entire life story, other times it's like extracting a confession.

The choice of illustrations in this book is as idiosyncratic as our meandering assignments. The process of choosing the subjects and art directing the illustrations in this book has been highly personal. That's us coming in to land at Mount Cook, that's us stuck in the traffic on the Auckland motorway, sipping the sauvignon in Marlborough and kicking around a ball at Mission Bay.

That's one of us running down the Mount aged 10 and the other on a bike on the Otago Rail Trail. That's neither of us bungying off the Kawarau Bridge. We've sung in the Waitomo Caves cathedral, we've scaled sun-burnt Te Mata Peak numerous times. And the most memorable place we've visited? Easy – Te Noho Kotahitanga Marae at Unitec, Point Chevalier. The whole New Zealand story captured in one stunning room.

We've been welcomed with warmth onto many marae and tried Cook Island dancing at friendly-as fono. We have come to appreciate that it's the Māori and Pacific peoples who truly set this country apart and that our increasingly cosmopolitan mix will be the making of us.

Over the years we've also roared on the All Blacks, the All Whites, the Black Caps, the Tall Blacks and more than our fair share of long-haired middle-distance runners. Experience has taught us that the national mood is perilously tied to the fortune of these people.

This scenic country is very kind to cameras but we wanted to capture something different, something about the spirit and quirkiness of the place. So here is our New Zealand. A place … where many of us won't wear a raincoat when it pours… where we persist with shorts in the cold… where the ratepayer is perpetually outraged … and where summer never fails to disappoint. Against all odds we are a nation of city slickers hanging on the price of milk-solids.

Yes, life in New Zealand is never less than entertaining and that's the spirit of this book. We're sorry we couldn't fit in all your wonderful suggestions. There's no Naseby, no Ongarue, no Hooper's inlet, no Hen and Chicken Islands.

And sorry Elizabeth, there's no Fairlie!

Arohanui

Michael Fitzsimons   **Nigel Beckford**

(aka FitzBeck)

AOTEAROA

NELSON

TASMAN

MARLBOROUGH

WEST COAST

CANTERBURY

OTAGO

SNOW

SOUTHLAND

STEWART
ISLAND

FOVEAUX
STRAIT

SOUTH ISLAND
TE WAI POUNAMU

MAUI'S BIG FISH

ACCORDING TO MYTHOLOGY, MAUI, A DEMIGOD FROM HAWAIKI, USED A MAGIC FISH HOOK TO REEL IN TE IKA A MAUI (THE NORTH ISLAND) FROM THE OCEAN DEPTHS. TE WAKA A MAUI (THE SOUTH ISLAND) WAS HIS CANOE AND TE PUNGA A MAUI (STEWART ISLAND) HIS ANCHOR. AN ARGUMENT AMONG MAUI'S BROTHERS TO CHOP UP THE CATCH CREATED THE MOUNTAINS AND VALLEYS OF THE LANDSCAPE. EVEN MORE IMPRESSIVELY, MAUI SLOWED DOWN THE SUN BECAUSE HE DIDN'T LIKE EATING HIS FOOD IN THE DARK -AN EARLY VERSION OF DAYLIGHT SAVING.

THE FIRST
VOYAGERS

ACCORDING TO TRADITION, POLYNESIAN EXPLORER KUPE WAS THE FIRST TO DISCOVER AOTEAROA AROUND 750AD. SOME TIME BETWEEN 1200 AND 1300 → A NUMBER OF WAKA HOURUA (VOYAGING CANOES) MADE THE EPIC JOURNEY, NAVIGATING BY THE STARS, FROM EAST POLYNESIA. SEVEN OF THEM – AOTEA, KURAHAUPŌ, MATAATUA, TAINUI, TOKOMARU, TE ARAWA AND TĀKITIMU – HOLD SPECIAL SIGNIFICANCE FOR MĀORI ANCESTRY TO THIS DAY.

Matariki

The Māori year is ushered in by the appearance of **Matariki** (the Seven Sisters Star cluster) just before dawn in the winter sky. According to Māori tradition, Matariki is a time to remember the dead, celebrate the harvest and new life and plan for the future. The Matariki festival is a popular event on the New Zealand social calendar.

EUROPEAN EXPLORERS

Dutch explorer, Abel Tasman, was the first European to reach New Zealand on the 13th December, 1642 on board the Zeehaven at Golden Bay. A hostile reception meant he never landed.

CAPTAIN JAMES COOK,

ABOARD THE ENDEAVOUR

SIGHTED POVERTY BAY ON THE EAST COAST ON THE 6TH OCTOBER, 1769.

OVER THE NEXT SIX MONTHS COOK MAPPED
THE WHOLE NEW ZEALAND COASTLINE.
HE RETURNED TWICE MORE TO THESE SHORES,
IN 1773 AND 1777, ABOARD THE RESOLUTION.

NICHOLAS YOUNG, THE SURGEON'S BOY,
SIGHTED THE COASTLINE OF NEW ZEALAND
FROM THE MASTHEAD OF THE ENDEAVOUR.

THE TREATY
— A LIVING DOCUMENT —

New Zealand's founding document, the Treaty of Waitangi, was signed on 6 February in <u>1840</u> between Māori chiefs and the Crown.

It handed the British sovereignty over the country in exchange for guaranteed Māori rights of ownership of their lands, forests, and fisheries.

The Treaty has been the basis for rancour and reconciliation in New Zealand race relations ever since.

Since 1975, more than 2,000 alleged breaches of the Treaty by the Crown have been lodged with the Waitangi Tribunal. By 2010 compensation of $950 million had been paid.

A further $1 billion of claims are pending.

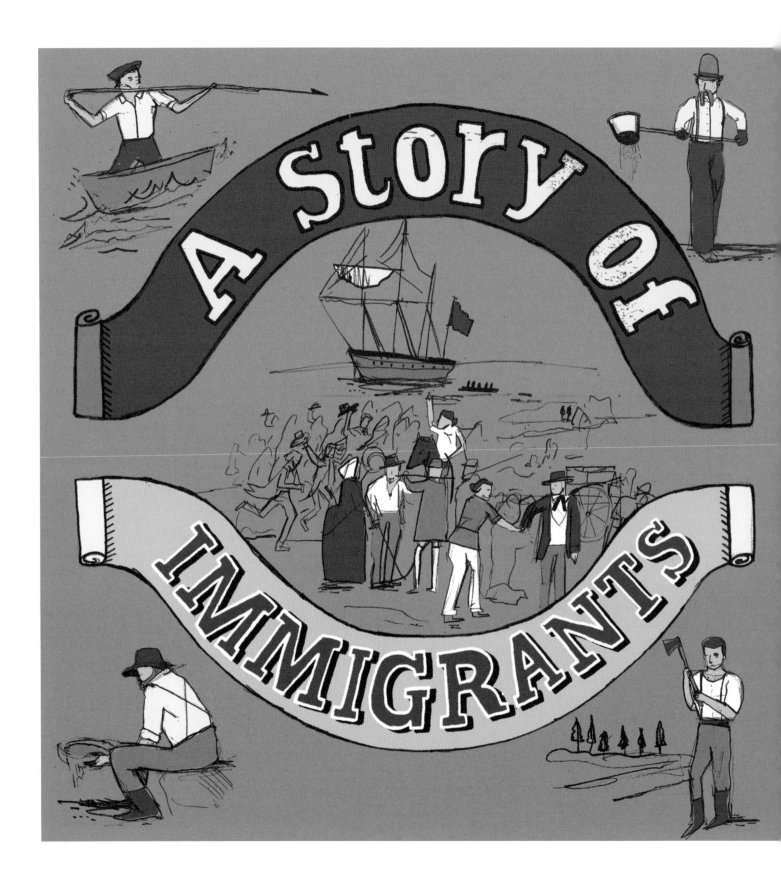

EUROPEANS BEGAN ARRIVING IN NEW ZEALAND FROM THE BEGINNING OF THE 19th CENTURY, DESPERATE FOR A FRESH START. FIRST TO COME WERE WHALERS AND SEALERS, THEN AGRICULTURAL WORKERS BROUGHT HERE UNDER COMPANY SETTLEMENT SCHEMES.

THE GOLD RUSH OF THE 1860s DREW MANY MORE THOUSANDS.

IN THE 20 YEARS FROM 1851 TO 1871, THE POPULATION GREW FROM 27,000 TO 255,000. BY 1916, THE TOTAL POPULATION TOPPED A MILLION.

MOST MIGRANTS WERE BRITISH UNTIL THE MID 20th CENTURY. SINCE THEN PEOPLE FROM THROUGHOUT THE PACIFIC AND ASIA HAVE SETTLED HERE IN LARGE NUMBERS. MORE RECENT NEWCOMERS FROM AFRICA AND THE MIDDLE EAST HAVE ADDED TO THE HYBRID VIGOUR OF THE NATION. THESE DAYS 1 IN 4 NEW ZEALANDERS WAS BORN OVERSEAS AND AUCKLAND IS HOME TO 150 ETHNIC COMMUNITIES.

WEST NEW ZEALAND

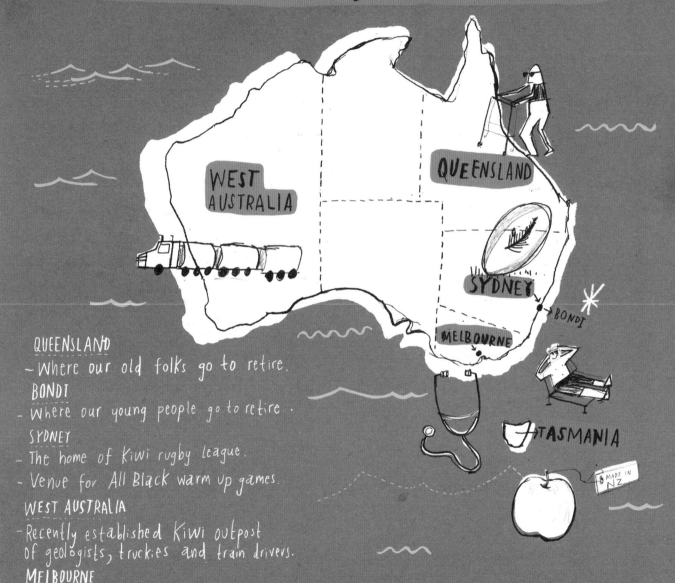

QUEENSLAND
- Where our old folks go to retire.

BONDI
- Where our young people go to retire.

SYDNEY
- The home of Kiwi rugby league.
- Venue for All Black warm up games.

WEST AUSTRALIA
- Recently established Kiwi outpost of geologists, truckies and train drivers.

MELBOURNE
- Where Kiwi doctors and nurses make their mistakes and learn.

TASMANIA
- Testing facility for New Zealand apples.

***AUSTRALIAN MUSIC AWARDS**
- Annual ceremony honouring New Zealand musicians

our people

our people

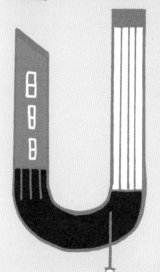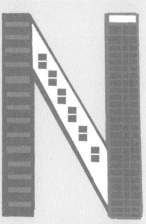

URBAN

SMALL-POPULATION 4.4 MILLION

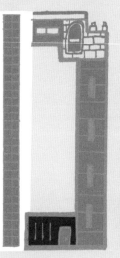

ISED

80%
LIVE IN CITIES

DIVERSE

67.6% EUROPEAN	9.2% ASIAN
14.4% MĀORI	6.9% POLYNESIAN

OUTNUMBERED

70 MILLION POSSUMS | 5.8 MILLION DAIRY COWS | 32 MILLION SHEEP

NATURAL

A THIRD OF THE COUNTRY IS PROTECTED IN NATIONAL PARKS AND RESERVES.

ISLANDERS

EVERYBODY LIVES WITHIN A 2 HOUR DRIVE FROM THE COAST.

EMPTY

ONLY 14 PEOPLE PER SQ KM.
(240 PER SQ KM IN UK)

OUR PEOPLE

ACCIDENT-PRONE

1 IN 7 PEOPLE WERE INJURED IN THEIR HOME LAST YEAR

DRIVEN

1 CAR FOR EVERY 2 PEOPLE

TECH SAVVY

85% HAVE A MOBILE PHONE, 75% OF HOUSEHOLDS HAVE INTERNET

HONEST RANKED LEAST CORRUPT COUNTRY ON EARTH

—GLOBAL CORRUPTION PERCEPTIONS INDEX

EXPERIMENTERS

FIRST TO GIVE WOMEN THE VOTE
IN THE 1890s, CHAMPIONS
OF THE WELFARE STATE IN THE
1930s, FREE MARKET ZEALOTS IN
THE 1980s.

PROGRESSIVE

MORE THAN A THIRD OF
PARLIAMENTARIANS ARE WOMEN.

POLITICAL INNOVATORS

CHANGED VOTING SYSTEM IN
1993 FROM FIRST PAST THE POST
TO MIXED MEMBER PROPORTIONAL
REPRESENTATION.

DEMOCRATIC

76% OF PEOPLE VOTE, HIGH
BY INTERNATIONAL STANDARDS.

✳ KATE SHEPPARD

A PACIFIC NATION

PACIFIC PEOPLES MAKE UP 7% OF NEW ZEALAND'S POPULATION AND ARE ESTIMATED TO BE 10% BY 2026. AUCKLAND HAS THE LARGEST PACIFIC POPULATION OF ANY CITY IN THE WORLD.

ONE OF THE HIGHLIGHTS OF THE RUGBY WORLD CUP WAS THE
BOUNDLESS ENTHUSIASM OF PACIFIC FANS FOR THEIR HOME NATIONS.

Gamma

Delta

Epsilon

Beta

Alpha

THE SOUTHERN CROSS

The Milky Way (Te Ikaroa) contains NEW ZEALAND's most celebrated constellation the SOUTHERN CROSS, and its two pointers, Alpha and Beta Centauri. For centuries, the constellation was used as a navigation→ aid (to find true SOUTH) by MAORI and EUROPEAN mariners. The four brightest STARS of the five star cross adorn NEW ZEALAND's FLAG, but the constellation actually comprises thousands of STARS. The brightest star (Acrux at the bottom of the cross) is actually a triple STAR, 321 light years from EARTH. The closest, Gamma Crux ↑ at the top, is just 88 light years away. Even on a ROCKET, your trip there would still take several MILLION years.

LAND OF THE LONG FLAT WHITE

ROASTER
CUPPING

AROMA
NATURAL FRUIT ACIDITY

$4

$3.50

COFFEE

DOUBLE SHOT

PROCESS

☐ SYPHON

CHEMEX

REGULAR ☑ LARGE ☐

FLAT WHITE

TRIM ☐   SOY ☑

MACCHIATO   ESPRESSO MOCHA
PICCOLO SHORT BLACK
L O N G BLACK
CAPPUCCINO LATTE

NEW ZEALAND HAS MORE COFFEE ROASTERS PER CAPITA THAN ANYWHERE IN THE WORLD! IN THE SPACE OF A COUPLE OF DECADES, KIWIS HAVE BECOME COFFEE CONNOISSEURS WITH EVEN THE SMALLEST TOWN BOASTING ITS OWN HIP BARISTA CULTURE.

TASTING NOTES:-

SINGLE ORIGIN
SPICY
COMPLEX

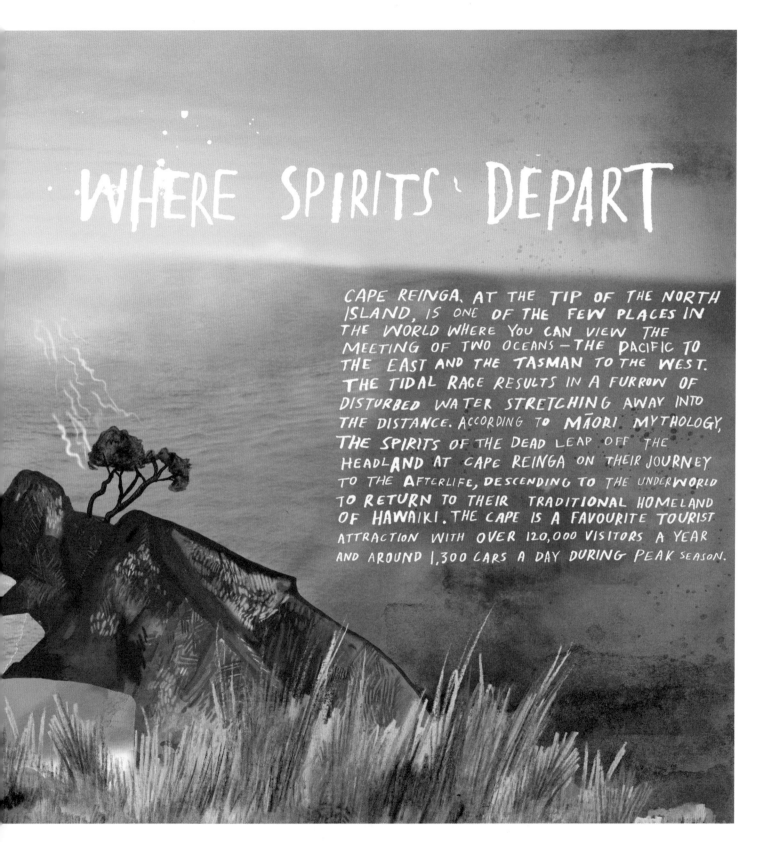

WHERE SPIRITS DEPART

CAPE REINGA, AT THE TIP OF THE NORTH ISLAND, IS ONE OF THE FEW PLACES IN THE WORLD WHERE YOU CAN VIEW THE MEETING OF TWO OCEANS — THE PACIFIC TO THE EAST AND THE TASMAN TO THE WEST. THE TIDAL RAGE RESULTS IN A FURROW OF DISTURBED WATER STRETCHING AWAY INTO THE DISTANCE. ACCORDING TO MĀORI MYTHOLOGY, THE SPIRITS OF THE DEAD LEAP OFF THE HEADLAND AT CAPE REINGA ON THEIR JOURNEY TO THE AFTERLIFE, DESCENDING TO THE UNDERWORLD TO RETURN TO THEIR TRADITIONAL HOMELAND OF HAWAIKI. THE CAPE IS A FAVOURITE TOURIST ATTRACTION WITH OVER 120,000 VISITORS A YEAR AND AROUND 1,300 CARS A DAY DURING PEAK SEASON.

90 MILE BEACH

NORTHLAND'S 90 MILE BEACH IS ACTUALLY ONLY 55 MILES LONG, BUT NO ONE FEELS SHORT-CHANGED. THIS VAST BEACH AND ITS SPECTACULAR SAND DUNES, STRETCHING FROM AHIPARA TO SCOTT POINT, HAVE WON OVER EVERYONE FROM SURFCASTERS LOOKING FOR SNAPPER TO HORSE TREKKERS AND FOUR WHEEL DRIVERS AFTER ADVENTURE.

THE BACH

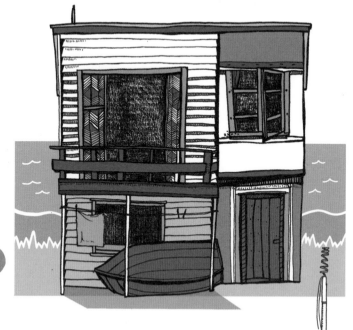

IN A COUNTRY OF CONSTANT COASTLINE THE SEASIDE BACH (CRIB TO SOUTHERNERS) HAS ACQUIRED MYTHIC STATUS. FOR YEARS, IT WAS A SYMBOL OF HOMEGROWN SIMPLICITY AND FREEDOM. THE PROPERTY BOOM IN COASTAL LAND IN THE 90s AND NOUGHTIES·'ABSOLUTE BEACHFRONT!' → MEANS THESE HUMBLE DWELLINGS HAVE BEEN JOINED BY MUCH RICHER NEIGHBOURS.

Tiara
OF THE
Queen City

THE AUCKLAND HARBOUR BRIDGE IS AN ICON OF NEW ZEALAND'S LARGEST CITY. THE BRIDGE TOOK FOUR YEARS TO BUILD AND WAS OPENED IN 1959 WITH JUST FOUR LANES FOR TRAFFIC. IT WAS A TOLL BRIDGE FOR MANY YEARS. IN 1969 TWO-LANE BOX GIRDER SECTIONS, KNOWN AS 'NIPPON CLIP-ONS' WERE ADDED TO EACH SIDE TO COPE WITH THE SWELLING VOLUME OF TRAFFIC MOVING BETWEEN THE CITY AND THE EVER-EXPANDING NORTHSHORE. ON A BUSY DAY, UP TO 180,000 CARS TRAVEL ACROSS THE EIGHT-LANE, 1020 METRE BRIDGE. WITH THE BRIDGE CLOSE TO CAPACITY THERE HAS BEEN TALK OF A SECOND HARBOUR CROSSING. A TUNNEL LINK EAST OF THE EXISTING BRIDGE IS CURRENTLY THE MOST LIKELY OPTION.

NEARLY A THIRD OF NEW ZEALANDERS LIVE IN AUCKLAND. IT IS THE ECONOMIC POWERHOUSE OF THE COUNTRY, DELIVERING NEARLY A THIRD OF THE GDP. DESPITE ITS MOTORWAY MAYHEM, IT HAS RETAINED ITS LEAFY, SUBURBAN CHARM, REGULARLY RANKING IN THE TOP 10 PLACES IN THE WORLD TO LIVE. AUCKLANDERS HAVE A LOVE AFFAIR WITH THE SEA, OWNING 135,000 YACHTS AND LAUNCHES - MORE BOATS PER CAPITA THAN ANY OTHER CITY IN THE WORLD. THE REGION SITS ON TOP OF A LARGE (DORMANT!) VOLCANIC FIELD - WHEREVER YOU ARE, YOU ARE NEVER FAR FROM A BMW AND A VOLCANIC SLOPE.

PIHA BEACH –
WHERE LIFEGUARDS ARE MOVIE STARS

THANKS TO THE TASMAN SEA'S BARRELLING SURF AND TREACHEROUS RIPS, THIS BLACK SAND, WEST COAST BEACH, 30K FROM AUCKLAND, IS SYNONYMOUS WITH REALITY TV SHOW PIHA RESCUE. ITS CENTREPIECE IS THE BEAUTIFUL LION ROCK, A 100 METRE TALL VOLCANIC FORMATION MILLIONS OF YEARS OLD. A WAR MEMORIAL AT ITS BASE COMMEMORATES LOCALS WHO SERVED IN TWO WORLD WARS.

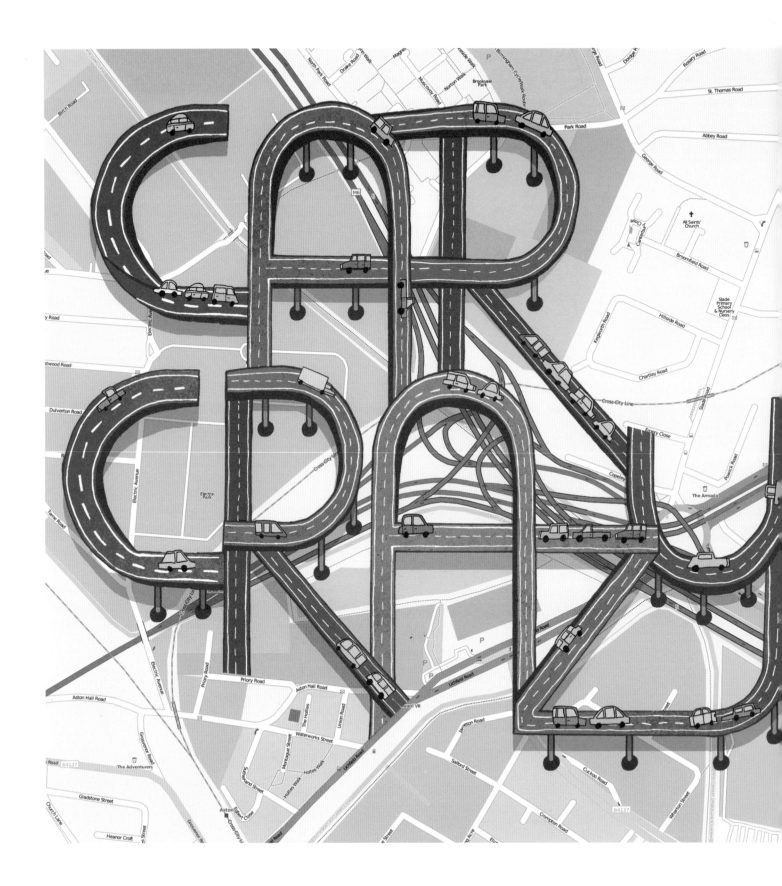

CITY OF WHEELS

VICTORIA PARK VIADUCT & TUNNEL   ALBANY   HIGHWAY

A vast motorway network in Auckland has

WESTERN RING ROAD   SOUTH WESTERN   MOTORWAY

fuelled an urban sprawl in all directions.

NEWMARKET VIADUCT REPLACEMENT   ELLERSLIE-PANMURE HIGHWAY

900,000-plus cars use the motorway

NORTHWEST   MOTORWAY   SOUTH-EASTERN   HIGHWAY

system each day, undeterred by lengthy,

NORTHERN MOTORWAY   MT WELLINGTON HIGHWAY

peak-hour traffic delays. More than 90%

                                        UPPER   HARBOUR MOTORWAY

of journeys are undertaken by car. Despite

        AUCKLAND HARBOUR CROSSING

                                        PAKURANGA   HIGHWAY

costly efforts to upgrade the rail & bus

        SOUTHERN   MOTORWAY

                                        ALBANY   EXPRESSWAY

system, public transport usage is very low

by international standards. WATERVIEW CONNECTION

        UPPER HARBOUR HIGHWAY

THE ALL BLACKS WERE CROWNED WORLD CHAMPIONS IN 2011, BEATING THE FRENCH BY A WHISKER IN THE RUGBY WORLD CUP FINAL. THE ALL BLACKS HAVE A PHENOMENAL WINNING RECORD, WINNING THREE-QUARTERS OF ALL THE GAMES THEY HAVE PLAYED SINCE 1903.

SPORTING FAIRYTALE

Fourth choice FIRST FIVE Stephen DONALD, RIDICULED by fans and overlooked by selectors, returned FROM THE wilderness IN a very tight Black Jersey to slot the winning goal (JUST!) IN the RUGBY WORLD CUP FINAL. In securing the All BLACKS their DESPERATELY sought-after second WORLD CUP VICTORY, DONALD became an INSTANT NATIONAL HERO.

MISSION BAY, NAMED AFTER THE MELANESIAN
MISSION ESTABLISHED BY BISHOP GEORGE SELWYN
IN 1848, IS A BUSTLING BEACH AREA IN AUCKLAND'S
WEALTHY EASTERN SUBURBS. PICNICERS AND BEACH-
LOVERS FLOCK TO THE PICTURESQUE BEACH RESERVE,
WHERE A GLORIOUS FOUNTAIN MADE OF SICILIAN MARBLE
AND FEATURING THREE BRONZE SEA MONSTERS, REGULARLY
GUSHES WATER 40 FEET INTO THE AIR. BEYOND THE
SHELLY BEACH LIES SYMMETRICAL RANGITOTO ISLAND,
AUCKLAND'S MOST ICONIC NATURAL FEATURE AND THE
MOST RECENTLY ACTIVE OF THE CITY'S VOLCANOES.
RANGITOTO WAS FORMED WITHIN THE LAST 1,000 YEARS.

MISSION BAY

THE STATE HOUSE

State Houses provide low-income Kiwi families with affordable rental accommodation. They were part of the Labour Government's groundbreaking welfare reforms of the 1930s. The first state house opened in Wellington in 1937. The country now has around 70,000. New Zealand's current Prime Minister John Key grew up in one in Christchurch.

HOT WATER BEACH

AROUND 13,000 VISITORS A YEAR FLOCK TO WORLD-FAMOUS HOT WATER BEACH ON THE EAST COAST OF THE COROMANDEL PENINSULA, 12 KILOMETRES SOUTHEAST OF WHITIANGA. FOR TWO HOURS EITHER SIDE OF LOW TIDE, YOU CAN DIG IN THE SAND FOR HOT SPRING WATER AND CREATE YOUR OWN SPA POOL. THE WATER, LOADED WITH COPIOUS AMOUNTS OF CALCIUM, POTASSIUM, FLUORINE, BROMINE AND SILICA, FILTERS UP FROM UNDERGROUND RESERVOIRS OF SUPERHEATED WATER VIA TWO UNDERGROUND FISSURES, REACHING TEMPERATURES AS HOT AS 64°C.

Auckland
SH1
Whitianga
Hauraki Gulf
SH25
Tairua
Hot Water Beach
SH2
SH25a

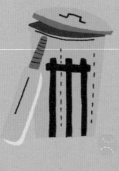

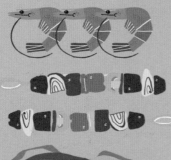

The gender divide is seldom more evident than at the traditional Kiwi 'barbie' where men and women part ways like the Red Sea before Moses. The men drink beer, tell stories and take turns at flipping the steaks while the women relish the no-fuss entertaining. Over the years the barbecue has become more sophisticated — the charcoal burner replaced with a state-of-the-art, stainless steel cooker and the humble sausage making way for fancy cuts of meat, exquisite seafood and gourmet salads. The barbie epitomises the easy-going New Zealand lifestyle and is often the focus of summer socialising.

Return to Middle-Earth

The Lord of the Rings' stunning success has created a state-of-the-art film and special effects industry in New Zealand and made Peter Jackson one of the most influential directors in the movie industry. LOTR is the highest grossing trilogy of all time - $2.91 billion - and was recognised with 17 Academy Awards. Now the stars are back in New Zealand for the filming of a 2-part adaptation of The Hobbit, a prequel to LOTR.

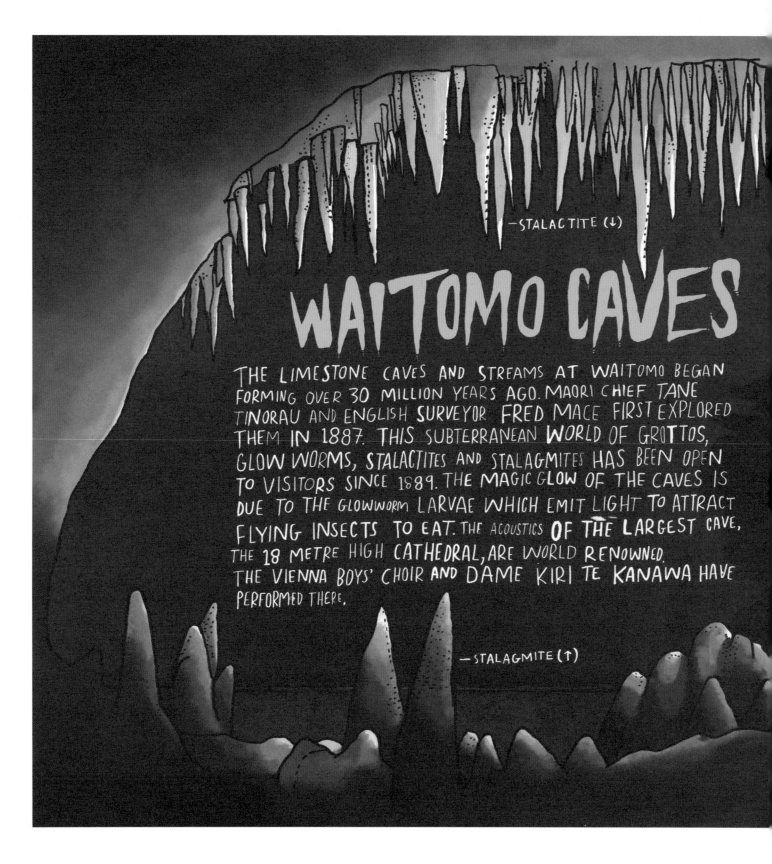

—STALACTITE (↓)

WAITOMO CAVES

THE LIMESTONE CAVES AND STREAMS AT WAITOMO BEGAN FORMING OVER 30 MILLION YEARS AGO. MAORI CHIEF TANE TINORAU AND ENGLISH SURVEYOR FRED MACE FIRST EXPLORED THEM IN 1887. THIS SUBTERRANEAN WORLD OF GROTTOS, GLOW WORMS, STALACTITES AND STALAGMITES HAS BEEN OPEN TO VISITORS SINCE 1889. THE MAGIC GLOW OF THE CAVES IS DUE TO THE GLOWWORM LARVAE WHICH EMIT LIGHT TO ATTRACT FLYING INSECTS TO EAT. THE ACOUSTICS OF THE LARGEST CAVE, THE 18 METRE HIGH CATHEDRAL, ARE WORLD RENOWNED. THE VIENNA BOYS' CHOIR AND DAME KIRI TE KANAWA HAVE PERFORMED THERE.

—STALAGMITE (↑)

* DAME KIRI TE KANAWA

WHITE GOLD

NEW ZEALAND IS THE COUNTRY WHERE THE FONTERRA MILK SOLID PAYOUT IS NATIONAL NEWS!! DAIRYING IS RESPONSIBLE FOR A MASSIVE 25% OF EXPORT EARNINGS & 1.5 MILLION HECTARES ARE DEVOTED TO IT. OUR LUSH PASTURES & FARMING KNOW-HOW COMBINE TO MAKE NEW ZEALAND A WORLD LEADER

IN DAIRYING. FONTERRA, OWNED BY 13,000 NEW ZEALAND DAIRY FARMERS, IS THE WORLD'S LARGEST EXPORTER OF DAIRY PRODUCTS.

MENU

FOR THREE HOURS EVERY FRIDAY NIGHT, MESSAGES ABOUT HEALTHY EATING FALL ON DEAF EARS, AS NEW ZEALANDERS QUEUE TO ORDER: BATTERED FISH, PAUA FRITTERS, HOT DOGS, CRAB STICKS, POTATO FRITTERS, PINEAPPLE RINGS, CRUMBED OYSTERS AND MULTIPLE SCOOPS OF CHIPS ACCOMPANIED BY LASHINGS OF SALT. NEW ZEALANDERS EAT $1 BILLION OF FAST FOOD EVERY YEAR AND FISH & CHIPS ARE STILL A FAVOURITE. THERE IS A HOTLY CONTESTED ANNUAL COMPETITION TO CHOOSE NEW ZEALAND'S BEST FISH & CHIP SHOP. MOST KIWIS HAVE A FAVOURITE WITHIN DRIVING DISTANCE.

New Zealand Seafood
A Healthy Future

FRESH FISH COOKED TO ORDER

POTATO FRITTERS 70¢

24 26 27

59

TIMBER!

NEARLY 7% (1.7 MILLION HECTARES) OF NZ IS COVERED IN PINE TREES (PINUS RADIATA)! HUGE INVESTMENT IN PINE FOREST PLANTATIONS FROM THE 1960s HAS CREATED A $5 BILLION INDUSTRY, NZ's THIRD BIGGEST EXPORT EARNER. PINE, PULP AND MILLING DRIVE THE FORTUNES OF TIMBER TOWNS LIKE TOKOROA, KAWERAU, MURUPARA AND KAINGAROA.

THE MOUNT

TAURANGA IS ONE OF NEW ZEALAND'S MOST POPULAR SUMMER HOLIDAY SPOTS AS WELL AS A THRIVING CONTAINER PORT. AT THE HARBOUR ENTRANCE, LOOMS THE 232 METRE, EXTINCT VOLCANO MAUAO, MOUNT MAUNGANUI, WHICH IS SACRED TO LOCAL IWI. IN 2008, OWNERSHIP OF MAUAO WAS TRANSFERRED FROM THE CROWN TO THE NGATI TE RANGI, NGATI RANGINUI AND NGATI PUKENGA IWI.

AT THE BASE OF THE MOUNT SITS A HOLIDAY PARK WHOSE BEACHFRONT CAMP SITES ARE IN HOT DEMAND.

61

FIRST TO SEE THE SUN*

THE EAST COAST IS SYNONYMOUS WITH SUMMER - BLUE SKIES, IDYLLIC BEACHES AND BAYS, MAIZE TALL IN THE FIELDS AND BAKING HOT TEMPERATURES. GISBORNE'S THE FIRST CITY IN NEW ZEALAND TO SEE THE SUN EVERY DAY AND ENJOYS OVER 2,200 HOURS OF SUN A YEAR. FARMING AND FORESTRY SUSTAIN THE REGION. IT WAS HERE EXPLORER CAPTAIN JAMES COOK FIRST LANDED IN NZ IN 1769. THE AREA HAS BEEN THE INSPIRATION FOR TWO OF NZ'S MOST POPULAR MOVIES WHALE RIDER & BOY.

* GISBORNE USED TO BE THE FIRST IN THE WORLD UNTIL SAMOA HOPPED OVER THE DATE-LINE IN 2011.

ROADWORKS

FULTON HOGAN'S 16 ASPHALT PLANTS ARE KEPT IN FULL PRODUCTION ON THE CONSTANT REPAIR OF NZ ROADS. IT'S HARD TO DRIVE A MILE WITHOUT ENCOUNTERING A STOP/GO SIGN, WITCHES CONES AND THE HI-VIS MEN AND WOMEN IN ORANGE.

RATS

DEVOURER OF NATIVE ANIMALS AND INSECTS.

RABBITS

THE PLAGUE OF SOUTH ISLANDERS.

POSSUMS

30 MILLION ARE RAVAGING NATIVE PLANTS, TREES AND BIRDS.

THE SUN

NZ'S LACK OF OZONE MEANS SKIN CANCER RATES ARE AMONG THE WORLD'S HIGHEST.

KNOW YOUR ENEMY!

PSA

BACTERIAL VINE DISEASE THREATENING OUR $1 BILLION KIWIFRUIT INDUSTRY.

VARROA MITE

HIVE-KILLING NEMESIS OF BEEKEEPERS.

DIDYMO

TOXIC ALGAE INVADING OUR WATERWAYS.

STOATS

CHIEF KILLER OF OUR NATIONAL BIRD, THE GROUND-HUGGING KIWI.

WEASELS & FERRETS

COUSIN OF THE STOAT. ENOUGH SAID.

BROTHERS AND SISTERS
IN THE WIND

NZ's LOVE AFFAIR WITH MOTORCYCLES TAKES MANY FORMS ENJOYED BY 65,000 RIDERS. THERE ARE MOTORCYCLE CLUBS RAISING MONEY FOR CHARITY; GANG MEMBERS SUCH AS THE DEVIL'S HENCHMEN & THE FILTHY FEW; BISHOP BRIAN TAMAKI ON HIS 'HARLEY-LUJAH' DAVIDSON AND **PORN KING** STEVE CROW WITH HIS 'BOOBS ON BIKES' ENTOURAGE.

ROTORUA IS NEW ZEALAND'S GEOTHERMAL TOURIST MECCA. THOUSANDS OF YEARS OF VOLCANIC UPHEAVAL HAVE LEFT THE AREA CRATERED WITH A MULTITUDE OF LAKES, MUDPOOLS, WHIRLPOOLS, HOT POOLS AND STEAMING GEYSERS. THE LARGEST GEYSER, POHUTU AT WHAKAREWAREWA, BLOWS 15 TIMES A DAY AND SPURTS NEARLY 28 METRES IN THE AIR. THE AREA'S ALSO FAMOUS FOR ITS TROUT FISHING AND 'EGGY', SULPHUROUS AROMAS.

LETTING OFF STEAM

BEST OF THE WEST

NEW PLYMOUTH MAKES THE MOST OF THE TASMAN SEA WITH A 10-KILOMETRE COASTAL WALKWAY. THE TOWN'S GOVETT BREWSTER ART GALLERY IS HOME TO WORLD-RENOWNED, KINETIC ARTIST LEN LYE'S COLLECTION.

A 45-METRE WIND WAND ON THE CITY'S FORESHORE CELEBRATES THIS. NEVER FAR FROM VIEW IS EVERYONE'S IDEA OF WHAT A VOLCANO SHOULD LOOK LIKE - THE SPLENDIDLY SPHERICAL, 2,518 METRE MT TARANAKI.

Talkin' it up!!

EVER SINCE COLONIAL TIMES WHEN NEW ZEALAND WAS DESCRIBED TO PROSPECTIVE IMMIGRANTS AS 'VERY NEAR TO AUSTRALIA', NEW ZEALANDERS HAVE FELT AN IRRESISTABLE URGE TO PROMOTE THEMSELVES WITH ICONS, BRANDS AND SLOGANS. IN SMALL TOWN NEW ZEALAND, IN PARTICULAR, THIS BOOSTERISM KNOWS NO BOUNDS.

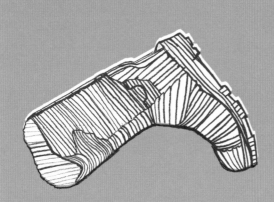

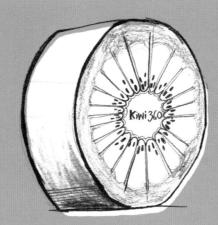

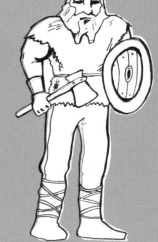

More than you expect
HAMILTON

So nice they named it twice
KERIKERI

Feel the heartbeat
TIMARU

You matter in Matamata
MATAMATA

Take a liking to a viking
DANNEVIRKE

Hawkes Bay's oldest inland town
WAIPAWA

Fox Town of New Zealand
FOXTON

2,000 ft above worry level
NASEBY

Whatever it takes
ASHBURTON

Good for the soul
COROMANDEL

Tempt me Tauranga
TAURANGA

Lotsa colour
WESTCOAST

We've got the lot
LOWER HUTT

City of knowledge
PALMERSTON NORTH

Live the day
NELSON

I am Dunedin
DUNEDIN

69

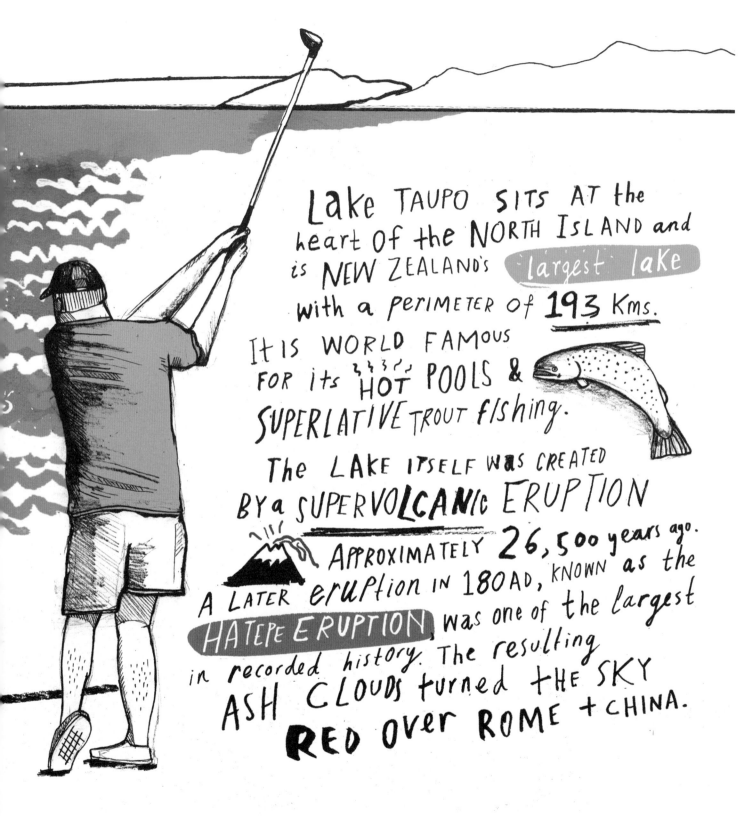

Lake TAUPO SITS AT the heart OF the NORTH ISLAND and is NEW ZEALAND's largest lake with a PERIMETER of **193** Kms.

It IS WORLD FAMOUS FOR its HOT POOLS & SUPERLATIVE TROUT fIshing.

The LAKE ITSELF was CREATED BY a SUPERVOLCANIC ERUPTION APPROXIMATELY **26,500** years ago. A LATER eruption IN 180 AD, KNOWN as the HATEPE ERUPTION, was one of the largest in recorded history. The resulting ASH CLOUDS turned tHE SKY RED OVER ROME + CHINA.

The Volcanic Plateau

THE JOURNEY ALONG STATE HIGHWAY ONE ACROSS THE LUNAR
LANDSCAPE OF THE DESERT ROAD IS ONE OF THE GREAT
NEW ZEALAND DRIVES. THE THREE ACTIVE PEAKS OF MT RUAPEHU,
NGAURUHOE AND TONGARIRO RISE MONUMENTALLY TO THE WEST.
THE ROAD DISSECTS A DESOLATE TUSSOCK PLAIN, CALLED THE RANGIPO
DESERT, AND IS REGULARLY CLOSED DURING HEAVY SNOW STORMS.
THIS HARSH ALPINE ENVIRONMENT, MUCH OF IT 1,000 METRES OR
MORE ABOVE SEA LEVEL, HAS SPARSE VEGETATION AND ICEY STREAMS
THAT GOUGE DEEP SERRATED VALLEYS THROUGH THE ASH AND RUST-RED
EARTH. PETER JACKSON FOUND IT THE PERFECT PLACE FOR THE
CLIMACTIC BATTLES OF MORDOR IN THE LORD OF THE RINGS FILMS,

ARMY TRAINING GROUP WAIOURU
LIVE FIRING,
& EXPLOSIONS
ANY TIME, BOTH SIDES OF ROAD

TE MATA PEAK

TE MATA PEAK TOWERS 400 METRES ABOVE
SEA LEVEL, OFFERING MARVELLOUS VIEWS OVER
HAWKE'S BAY. ON A CLEAR DAY YOU CAN SEE AS
FAR AS MT RUAPEHU & THE MAHIA PENINSULA.
MULTITUDES OF VISITORS REGULARLY HIKE, BIKE
OR DRIVE UP THE PEAK WHILE THE MORE
ADVENTUROUS RISK EVERYTHING BY LEAPING OFF
THE PEAK ON FLIMSY HANG-GLIDERS.

THIS GOLDEN SAND
BAY BEACH IS STEEPED BACK
HISTORY DATING BACK
EARLIEST POLYNESIAN
EXPLORERS.

"HAWKES"
IN MAORI
TO THE

ACCORDING TO TRADITION, THE TAKITIMU CANOE
TRIBE NGATI
(ANCESTRAL CANOE OF LOCAL
KAHUNGUNGU) LANDED HERE, ONE OF THE
SEVEN MIGRATION (350°
HAWAIKI AROUND TO VOYAGE FROM
MEANS 'MOON ON THE
THE BEACH AND A
BARE ISLAND ON A
MAKE SPECTACULAR

WAIMARAMA
O THE WATER: AND
MOTU O KURA/
MOONLIT NIGHT
VIEWING.

WAIMARAMA BEACH

ACCORDING TO LEGEND, MOTU O KURA WAS USED AS A SANCTUARY BY LOCAL MĀORI FROM INVADING TRIBES AND IS NAMED AFTER 'KURA,' A WOMAN WHO GATHERED FRESH WATER FROM A SEABED SPRING WHEN THE ISLAND WAS UNDER SIEGE.

LAND OF THE LOST

NEW ZEALANDERS' LOVE OF THE GREAT OUTDOORS AND LAID-BACK ATTITUDE TO RISK HAVE ENSURED A THRIVING SEARCH & RESCUE INDUSTRY. IN 2010 POLICE, COASTGUARD, TRAMPERS, MOUNTAINEERS, MARINERS, AVIATORS, MILITARY PERSONNEL AND VOLUNTEERS ATTENDED 2,374 SEARCH & RESCUE INCIDENTS—AN AVERAGE OF SIX AND A HALF A DAY! 630 PEOPLE WERE RESCUED.

The Lifestyle Block

Since the 1980s, the lure of country living has led large numbers of kiwis to abandon the suburbs for the lifestyle block - hobby farms on the outskirts of town. It is estimated that there are over 100,000 lifestyle farms. Nearly half a million hectares of former pasture land have been subdivided to cater for a threefold increase in small block holders in the past decade. 'Lifestylers' range from boutique farmers seeking a return, to weekend hobbyists doing an honest day's lambing, calving, barn building, chicken rearing, fencing, irrigating and tree planting.

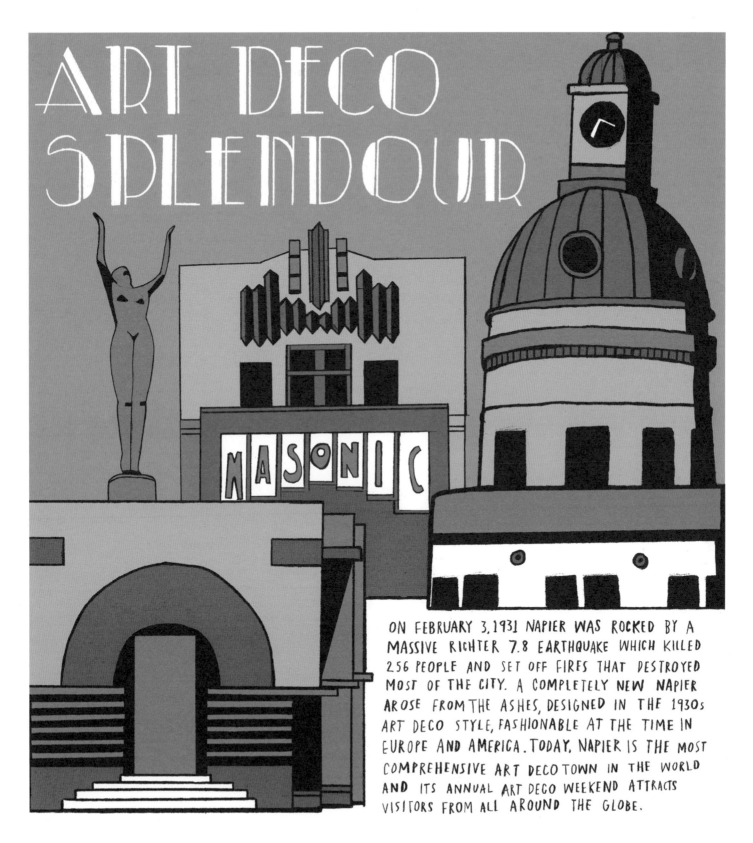

ART DECO SPLENDOUR

MASONIC

ON FEBRUARY 3, 1931 NAPIER WAS ROCKED BY A MASSIVE RICHTER 7.8 EARTHQUAKE WHICH KILLED 256 PEOPLE AND SET OFF FIRES THAT DESTROYED MOST OF THE CITY. A COMPLETELY NEW NAPIER AROSE FROM THE ASHES, DESIGNED IN THE 1930s ART DECO STYLE, FASHIONABLE AT THE TIME IN EUROPE AND AMERICA. TODAY, NAPIER IS THE MOST COMPREHENSIVE ART DECO TOWN IN THE WORLD AND ITS ANNUAL ART DECO WEEKEND ATTRACTS VISITORS FROM ALL AROUND THE GLOBE.

COOLEST LITTE CAPITAL

THE SWOOP DOWN NGAURANGA GORGE OUT ONTO WELLINGTON'S HARBOUR EDGE IS ONE OF THE MOST DRAMATIC APPROACHES TO A CITY YOU WILL FIND ANYWHERE. ACROSS THE WATER LIES SCENIC ORIENTAL BAY AND TO THE RIGHT A HIGH-RISE CITYSCAPE SET INTO THE HILLS.
IN 2011 LONELY PLANET CALLED WELLINGTON THE 'COOLEST LITTLE CAPITAL IN THE WORLD.'

BEES ROUND THE HONEYPOT

WELLINGTON IS HOME TO AN ARMY OF PUBLIC SERVANTS. NO OTHER STREET IN NEW ZEALAND CAN COMPARE WITH THE TERRACE WHERE PUBLIC SERVICE MANDARINS IN FINE SUITS BUZZ FROM CAFÉ TO CAFÉ AND MEETING TO MEETING LIKE BEES AROUND A MINISTERIAL HONEYPOT.
THE ALL-POWERFUL TREASURY IS AT Nº1 THE TERRACE, JUST A STONE'S THROW FROM NEW ZEALAND'S PARLIAMENT AND THE CONE-SHAPED BEEHIVE.

THE TERRACE

MOJO

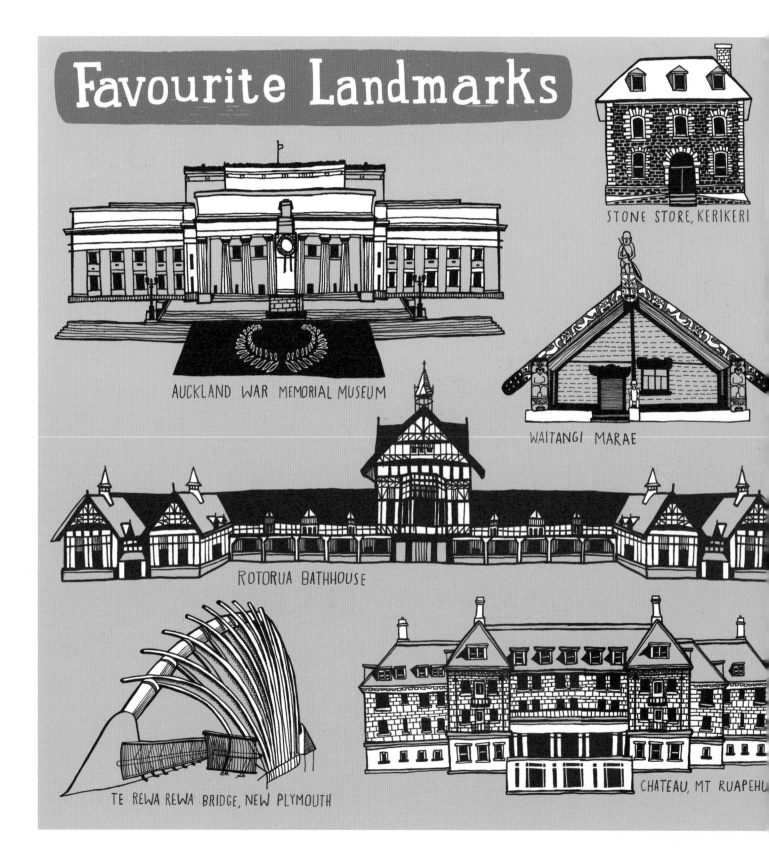

Favourite Landmarks

STONE STORE, KERIKERI

AUCKLAND WAR MEMORIAL MUSEUM

WAITANGI MARAE

ROTORUA BATHHOUSE

TE REWA REWA BRIDGE, NEW PLYMOUTH

CHATEAU, MT RUAPEHU

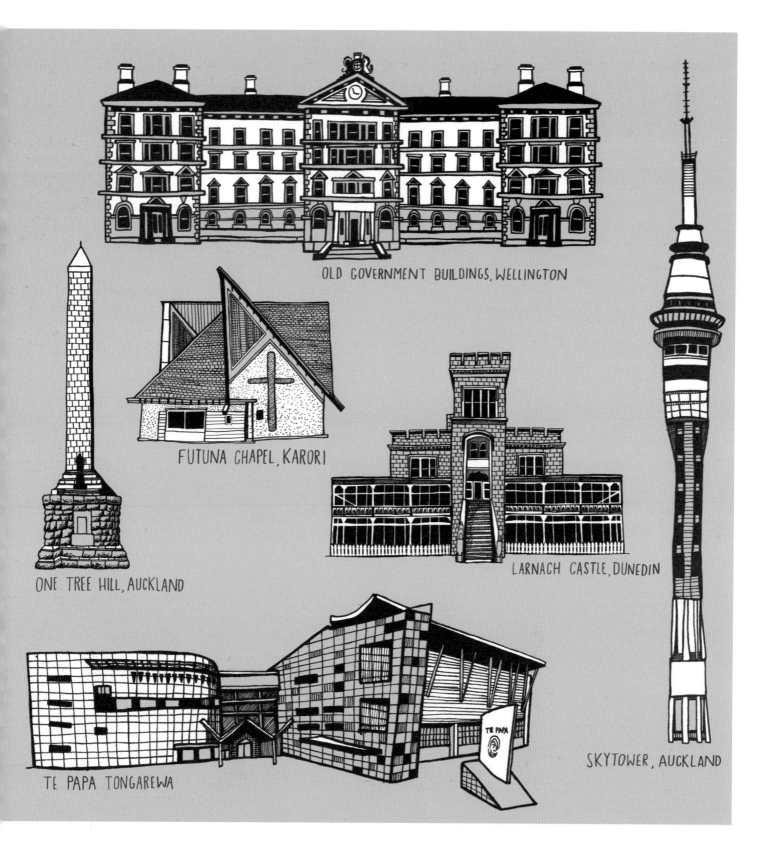

ONE TREE HILL, AUCKLAND

FUTUNA CHAPEL, KARORI

OLD GOVERNMENT BUILDINGS, WELLINGTON

LARNACH CASTLE, DUNEDIN

TE PAPA TONGAREWA

TE PAPA

SKYTOWER, AUCKLAND

THE CORNER DAIRY

THE CORNER DAIRY IS A FEATURE OF MOST NEW ZEALAND SUBURBS, SELLING ALL THE EVERYDAY ITEMS NEEDED TO KEEP YOUR HOUSE GOING, FROM GROCERIES & VEGIES TO TOILETRIES & THE NEWSPAPER. PRICES ARE HIGHER THAN AT THE SUPERMARKET BUT THESE NO-NONSENSE BUSINESSES SURVIVE DUE TO THEIR CONVENIENCE. THE CORNER DAIRY IS A FAVOURITE GATHERING PLACE FOR YOUNG TEENAGERS WITH TIME ON THEIR HANDS.

89

COOK STRAIT.

PELORUS JACK THE DOLPIN
-1888 -1912 -GONE BUT NOT FORGOTTEN

interislander
WWW.INTERISLANDER.CO.NZ

SOUTH WELLINGTON
POETRY CLUB.

COOK STRAIT IS ONE OF THE TRICKIEST AND MOST DANGEROUS STRETCHES OF WATER IN THE WORLD. THE 'ROARING FORTIES' AND SOUTHERLY STORMS CAN TURN IT FROM MILLPOND TO MOUNTAINOUS SWELL WITHIN HOURS. THE STRAIT'S NAMED AFTER CAPT. JAMES COOK WHO SAILED THROUGH IT IN 1770. A FERRY SERVICE BEGAN IN 1962 - A GOOD CROSSING TAKES AROUND 3 HOURS, A ROUGH ONE IN WILD WEATHER UP TO DOUBLE THAT. AT ITS NARROWEST POINT, THE STRAIT IS 23KM. THE FIRST PERSON TO SWIM IT, BARRIE DEVENPORT, TOOK 11 HRS AND 13 MINS IN 1962. THE CURRENT TIME TO BEAT IS 4 HRS, 37 MINS.

BARRIE DEVENPORT

BLENHEIM

KAIKOURA

CHRISTCHURCH

ASHBURTON

TIMARU

BLUFF

DUNEDIN

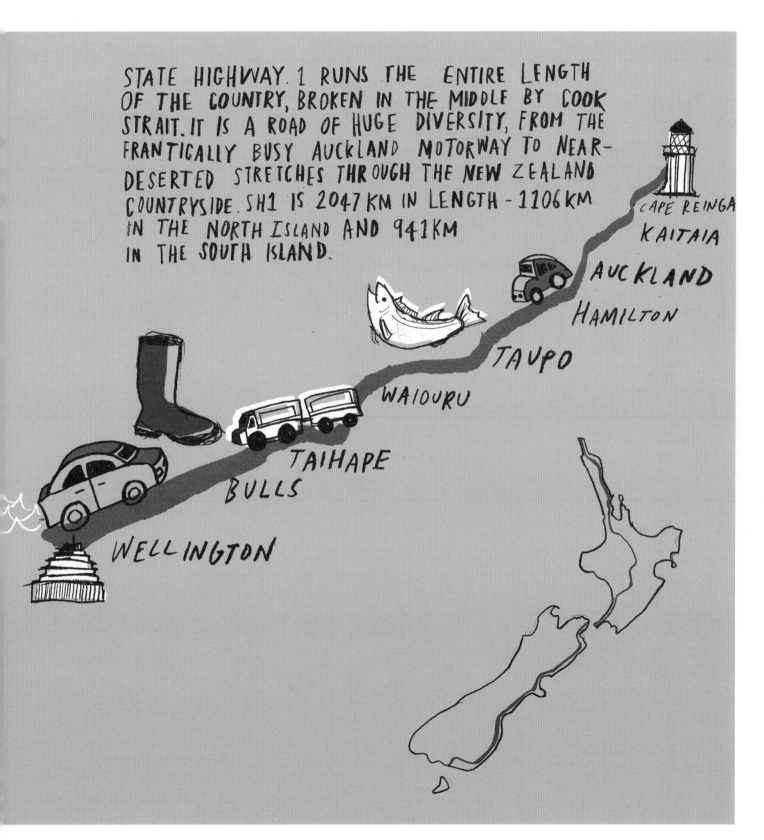

STATE HIGHWAY. 1 RUNS THE ENTIRE LENGTH OF THE COUNTRY, BROKEN IN THE MIDDLE BY COOK STRAIT. IT IS A ROAD OF HUGE DIVERSITY, FROM THE FRANTICALLY BUSY AUCKLAND MOTORWAY TO NEAR-DESERTED STRETCHES THROUGH THE NEW ZEALAND COUNTRYSIDE. SH1 IS 2047 KM IN LENGTH - 1106 KM IN THE NORTH ISLAND AND 941 KM IN THE SOUTH ISLAND.

CAPE REINGA
KAITAIA
AUCKLAND
HAMILTON
TAUPO
WAIOURU
TAIHAPE
BULLS
WELLINGTON

THE SOUNDS

The MARLBOROUGH SOUNDS WERE CREATED 12,000 YEARS AGO IN THE ICE AGE, WHEN SEA WATER FLOODED RIVER VALLEYS. THIS VAST NETWORK (4,000 SQUARE KILOMETRES) OF SHELTERED WATERWAYS, CHANNELS AND COVES NOW MAKE UP A FIFTH OF NEW ZEALAND'S COASTLINE. THE INTERISLAND FERRY GLIDES ITS WAY TO PICTON THROUGH TORY CHANNEL IN QUEEN CHARLOTTE SOUND. THE AREA IS ALSO FAMOUS FOR ITS COASTAL FOREST WALKS, NOTABLY THE QUEEN CHARLOTTE TRACK WHICH BEGINS AT SHIP COVE WHERE CAPTAIN COOK TOOK SHELTER IN 1770.

THE PUNGENT, ZESTY TASTE OF MARLBOROUGH SAUVIGNON
BLANC (FROM THE FRENCH "SAUVAGE" AND "BLANC") HAS PUT
NEW ZEALAND ON THE GLOBAL WINE MAP. PLANTINGS
BEGAN IN MARLBOROUGH IN THE 1970s, AND THE
REGION NOW PRODUCES NEARLY 80% OF NEW ZEALAND
WINES & TWO THIRDS OF OUR SAUVIGNON. MARLBOROUGH
SAUVIGNON BLANC IS OUR STAR PERFORMER INTERNATIONALLY,
AND IS RECOGNISED AS SETTING THE STANDARD FOR
THE VARIETY.

Golden BAY

EVER SINCE DUTCH EXPLORER ABEL TASMAN DROPPED ANCHOR HERE IN 1642, VISITORS HAVE BEEN DRAWN TO THE BREATHTAKING BEAUTY OF GOLDEN BAY. SEPARATED FROM THE REST OF THE SOUTH ISLAND BY STEEP HILL COUNTRY, GOLDEN BAY HAS IT ALL - ALPINE MEADOWS, FRESH-WATER SPRINGS, LIMESTONE CAVES, WORLD-CLASS HIKING TRACKS AND A STRING OF GOLDEN BAYS AND BEACHES. THE ABEL TASMAN COASTAL TRACK IS ONE OF NEW ZEALAND'S GREAT WALKS.

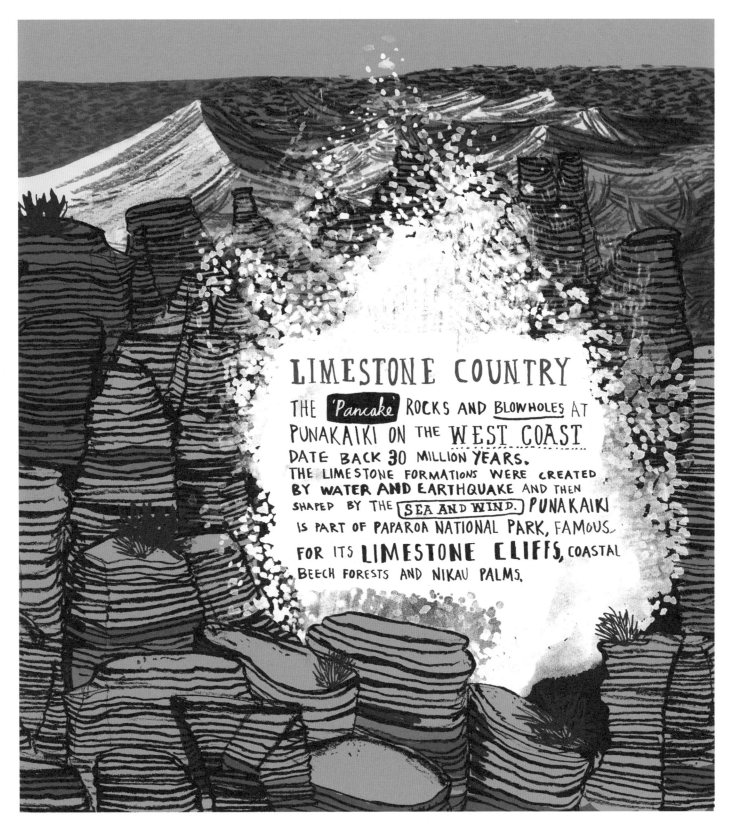

LIMESTONE COUNTRY

THE 'Pancake' ROCKS AND BLOWHOLES AT PUNAKAIKI ON THE WEST COAST DATE BACK 30 MILLION YEARS. THE LIMESTONE FORMATIONS WERE CREATED BY WATER AND EARTHQUAKE AND THEN SHAPED BY THE SEA AND WIND. PUNAKAIKI IS PART OF PAPAROA NATIONAL PARK, FAMOUS FOR ITS LIMESTONE CLIFFS, COASTAL BEECH FORESTS AND NIKAU PALMS.

WHITEBAITING

THE RESTFUL RITUAL OF SETTING NETS, SITTING ON A RIVER BANK AND WAITING FOR THE NEXT WHITEBAIT RUN HAS BEEN DESCRIBED AS MORE ADDICTIVE THAN SEARCHING FOR GOLD. THE 50mm-LONG FISH ARE PRIZED THROUGHOUT NEW ZEALAND AS A MYSTERIOUS AND REFINED DELICACY. WHITEBAIT HATCH IN FRESH WATER AND ARE THEN SWEPT OUT TO SEA WHERE THEY SPEND SEVERAL MONTHS BEFORE RETURNING TO THE RIVERS IN SPRING.

·BEST· WHITEBAIT FRITTERS

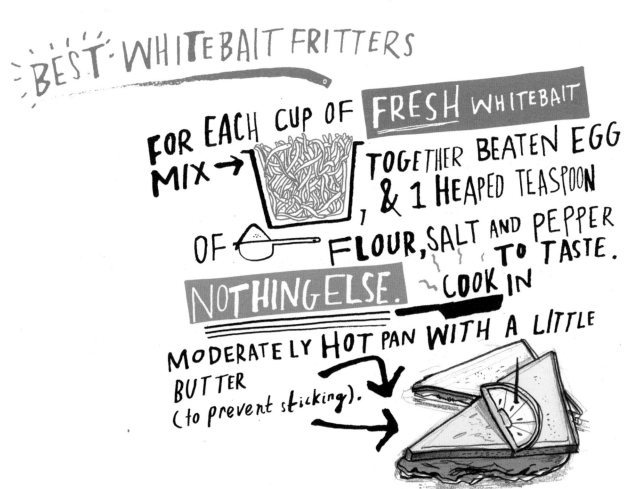

FOR EACH CUP OF FRESH WHITEBAIT MIX → TOGETHER BEATEN EGG & 1 HEAPED TEASPOON OF FLOUR, SALT AND PEPPER TO TASTE. NOTHING ELSE. COOK IN MODERATELY HOT PAN WITH A LITTLE BUTTER (to prevent sticking).

THE GREAT WALKS

WHANGANUI JOURNEY ABEL TASMAN COAST TRACK

ROUTEBURN TRACK TONGARIRO NORTHERN CIRCUIT

RAKIURA TRACK, STEWART ISLAND LAKE WAIKAREMOANA TRACK

MILFORD TRACK KEPLER TRACK HEAPHY TRACK,

THE NEW ZEALAND WILDERNESS HAS IRRESISTABLE APPEAL TO KIWIS AND TOURISTS ALIKE. THERE IS A VAST ARRAY OF TRAMPING TRACKS THROUGHOUT NEW ZEALAND BUT 9 GREAT WALKS HAVE BEEN IDENTIFIED, OFFERING ACCESS TO SOME OF THE BEST SCENERY IN THE COUNTRY. THESE WALKS TRAVERSE THE VOLCANIC PLATEAU, BEACHES, RAINFOREST, FJORDS & MOUNTAIN RANGES. THE MOST FAMOUS OF THEM, THE MILFORD TRACK, IS COMMONLY CALLED THE FINEST WALK IN THE WORLD.

THE **WILD FOOD** FESTIVAL

Hokitika's WILD FOOD Festival caters for CULINARY DAREDEVILS prepared to feast on HUHU grubs, STALLION semen, grasshoppers, SEAGULL EGGS and scorpions. 10,000 CURIOUS DINERS attend EACH YEAR.

THE WORLD'S LARGEST CARNIVORE

THE PRESENCE OF GIANT SPERM WHALES IN THE PACIFIC OCEAN WATERS OFF THE COAST OF KAIKOURA HAS TRANSFORMED THE SLEEPY SEASIDE TOWN INTO A MAJOR ECO-TOURISM DESTINATION, ATTRACTING 100,000 WHALE WATCHERS A YEAR. DEPENDING ON THE SEASON, WHALE WATCHERS CAN ALSO SEE HUMPBACK WHALES, PILOT WHALES BLUE WHALES AND SOUTHERN RIGHT WHALES AS WELL AS DOLPHINS AND SEALS.

THE COAST-TO-COAST RACE

This GUT-Busting ENDURANCE Race from KUMARA beach on the WEST coast to SUMNER beach in CHRISTCHURCH attracts Around 800 entries a YEAR. Competitors CYCLE, run and KAYAK the 243 kilometre traverse IN ALL WEATHERS across FORMIDABLE RIVERS, GORGES and MOUNTAINS. The fastest do IT IN UNDER 11 hours.

FINISH

9-time winning legend STEVE GURNEY

ROBIN JUDKINS

OPO AND MOKO
THE BOTTLENOSE DOLPHINS

SHREK

SIROCCO THE KAKAPO

RICHIE McCOW

PHAR LAP

CELEBRITY ANIMALS

KELLY THE DOLPHIN

PADDY THE WANDERER

HAPPY FEET

OPO AND MOKO THE BOTTLENOSE DOLPHINS

Opo's antics delighted holidaymakers in Hokianga harbour in the summer of 1955 and '56. Fifty-one years later, Moko did the same for residents in Mahia and Whakatane.

RICHIE McCOW

A black calf from Maungaturoto, Northland (pop. 837) purported to have 'psychic' powers to predict the outcome of All Blacks Rugby World Cup games.

PADDY THE WANDERER

A red Irish terrier who befriended watersiders and seamen on Wellington's wharves during the 1930s. He was farewelled with a 12-car funeral procession in 1939.

SIROCCO THE KAKAPO

This flightless, native parrot, one of only 124 left alive, is New Zealand's official 'Spokesbird' for conservation.

SHREK

New Zealand's most famous sheep was a high country, fugitive merino who evaded muster long enough to sport a massive 27 kilo fleece of wool.

KELLY THE DOLPHIN

The hoop-leaping star of Napier's Marineland for 34 years. Kelly's passing signalled the end of the iconic attraction.

PHAR LAP

Phar Lap, a chestnut gelding from Timaru, is New Zealand's most famous thoroughbred. He blitzed all-comers in the late twenties and thirties winning the Melbourne Cup and 36 other races.

HAPPY FEET

An emperor penguin from Antarctica who washed up on the Kapiti coast. Locals donated $7,000 worth of fish shakes and refrigeration to keep him alive.

CHRISTCHURCH-

CHRISTCHURCH IS FAMOUS FOR THE ENGLISHNESS OF ITS GARDENS, PARKS AND BUILDINGS, ITS LANDMARK CATHEDRAL AND MAIN SQUARE AND ACTIVITIES LIKE PUNTING ON THE **AVON**. ALL THAT CHANGED ON 4 SEPTEMBER 2010 AND 22 FEBRUARY 2011 WHEN DEVESTATING EARTHQUAKES CAUSED WIDESPREAD DAMAGE TO THE CITY. THE FEBRUARY QUAKE CLAIMED OVER 180 LIVES.

GET WELL SOON

A $20 BILLION REBUILDING EFFORT IS UNDERWAY. CANTABRIANS ARE RESILIENT AND HAVE RISEN MIGHTILY TO THE CHALLENGE - WITNESS THE 10,000 STRONG ARMY OF STUDENT VOLUNTEERS WHO SWUNG INTO ACTION IN THE QUAKE'S AFTERMATH, THE RAPID RE-OPENING OF SCHOOLS AND SHOPS AND AN AMBITIOUS REDEVELOPMENT PLAN FOR THE INNER CITY.

Hagley Park

Hagley Park is the green heart of Christchurch, our Garden City. The 165 hectare park was created in 1855 from swamp and scrub. It was named after the estate of the Chairman of the Canterbury Association, Lord Lyttelton. The park's exotic trees, botanic gardens, walking paths and setting by the Avon River evoke an unmistakable Englishness to this day.

KIWIANA

kiwis now celebrate their New Zealandness with all manner of kiwi memorabilia.

THE SOUTHERN ALPS

NEW ZEALAND's HIGHEST (AORAKI/MT COOK - 3,754) métres & LONGEST (450 Kms) MOUNTAIN RANGE RUNS ALONG THE SPINE OF THE ↓SOUTH ISLAND, DIVIDING ITS →EAST & WEST COASTS. THE SNOW-COVERED ALPS WERE FORMED OVER THE LAST 45 MILLION YEARS BY THE COLLISION OF TWO TECTONIC PLATES —THE PACIFIC and the INDO-AUSTRALIAN. THE ALPS CONTAIN NUMEROUS LAKES, 3,000 glaciers & THREE MOUNTAIN PASSES—THE LEWIS, ARTHUR & HAAST.

THE GREAT ESCAPE

COME THE WINTER WEEKENDS, LEGIONS OF SKIERS AND SNOW-BOARDERS FLEE THE CITIES TO ENJOY THE SPLENDOUR OF NEW ZEALAND'S RENOWNED SKI FIELDS. THERE ARE 42 SKI FIELDS IN 12 SKI REGIONS SPREAD ACROSS THE NORTH AND SOUTH ISLANDS.

A REMARKABLE TOWN

Postcard-perfect Queenstown is one of New Zealand's most popular tourist destinations. Set on the shores of Lake Wakatipu against the backdrop of the (truly) Remarkable mountain range, reaching up to 2,300 metres, Queenstown boasts fabulous scenic views. The alpine resort has become a mecca for skiers and adventure tourists the world over. Nearly two million visitors flock there every year to ski, snow board, luge, cable car, jet boat, horse trek and bungy jump. A thriving bar and restaurant scene takes care of any down time.

OTAGO TRAIL RAIL

EVERY YEAR AROUND 12,000 PEOPLE RIDE THE 150KM CENTRAL OTAGO RAIL TRAIL. THE HISTORIC TRAIL FOLLOWS AN ARC BETWEEN MIDDLEMARCH & CLYDE, ALONG THE GLORIOUS HIGHLAND ROUTE OF THE FORMER CENTRAL OTAGO RAILWAY. FOLLOWING THE CLOSURE OF THE RAILWAY IN 1993, THE **RAIL TRAIL** WAS CREATED & OPENED IN **2000**, BRINGING A NEW LEASE OF LIFE TO **THE AREA**. THE **DRAMATIC** RIDE TRAVERSES MOUNTAINS, PLAINS AND GORGES NOT SEEN FROM THE HIGHWAY.

WEDDERBURN

PASSPORT
OTAGO
AURIPO
WAIPIATA
HYDE

The Moeraki Bowling Club

THE WORLD-FAMOUS MOERAKI BOULDERS ON THE OTAGO COAST ARE MUDSTONE SPHERES CREATED 60 MILLION YEARS AGO ON THE SEA FLOOR. THEY WERE UNCOVERED FROM NEARBY CLIFFS AND SHAPED BY WIND AND SEA OVER THE YEARS.

SATURDAY MORNING SPORT.

Many Kiwi parents will never know the pleasure of a Saturday morning lie in. Instead..they are checking sports draws, listening to cancellations, organising transport and scouring maps for obscure sports fields. Then they line up in their thousands for hours on end to yell themselves hoarse supporting their kids. Over 800,000 kiwis volunteer their time to support sport and recreation in NZ.

FOX GLACIER

A 13 KILOMETRE-LONG RIVER OF ICE THAT STRETCHES FROM
THE BASE OF THE SOUTHERN ALPS TO THE RAIN FORESTS OF THE
WEST COAST. NAMED AFTER 19th CENTURY PRIME MINISTER,
SIR WILLIAM FOX, THE GLACIER IS PART OF WESTLAND'S TAI
POUTINI NATIONAL PARK AND A POPULAR TOURIST ATTRACTION.
NEARBY, LIES THE EQUALLY IMPRESSIVE, BUT SLIGHTLY SMALLER,
FRANZ JOSEF GLACIER.

Mitre Peak

MITRE PEAK IS ONE OF THE MOST PHOTOGRAPHED PARTS OF NEW ZEALAND. MILFORD SOUND AND ITS FAMOUS PEAK HAVE GRACED EVERYTHING FROM BISCUIT TINS AND TEA TOWELS TO MOUSE PADS IN THE NAME OF NATIONAL PRIDE. THE 1,692 METRE PEAK IS SHAPED LIKE A BISHOP'S MITRE AND ATTRACTS ALMOST AS MANY TOURISTS AS SAND FLIES. THE PEAK'S MIRROR IMAGE IN THE STILL WATERS OF THE SOUNDS IS A WONDER TO BEHOLD.

THIS 3-DAY, BIENNIAL EVENT IS A MUST FOR AVIATION Nostalgia buffs. LOVINGLY-RESTORED FIGHTERS & BOMBERS, SOME DATING BACK TO WORLD WAR ONE, Take PART IN AN AIRSHOW IN THE SKIES above WANAKA, IN CENTRAL OTAGO

AROUND 65,000 VISITORS ATTEND.

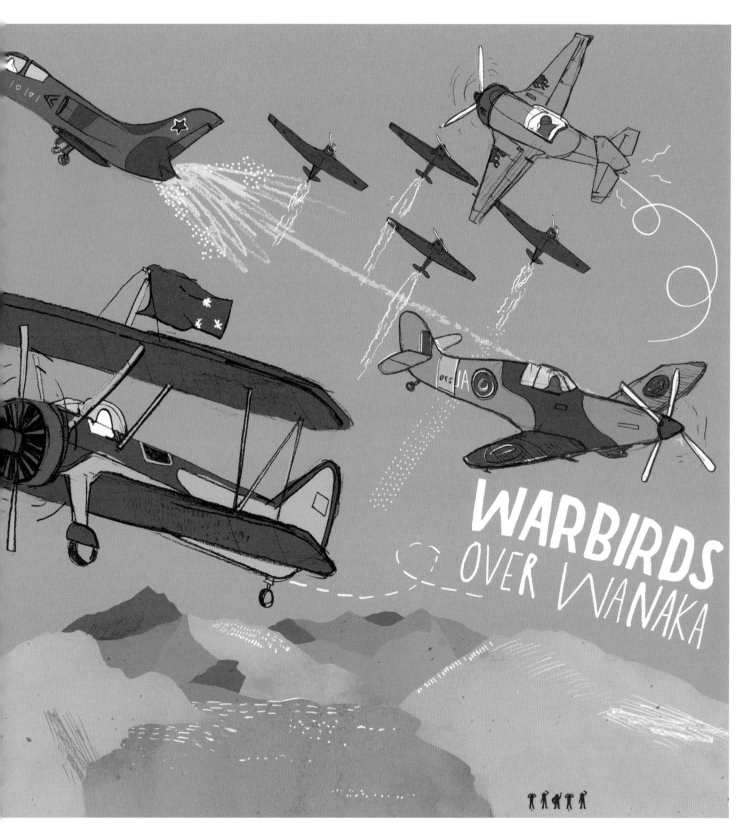

WARBIRDS OVER WANAKA

SCARFIES

DUNEDIN IS THE ULTIMATE STUDENT TOWN IN NEW ZEALAND, WITH ONE IN FIVE RESIDENTS A STUDENT. EVERY YEAR A LARRIKIN STUDENT STREAK PROVIDES A RICH VEIN OF ENTERTAINMENT FOR THE RESIDENT POPULATION. TOMORROW'S LAWYERS, ENGINEERS AND DOCTORS ARE TODAY'S REVELLERS, RIOTERS AND NUDE RUGBY PLAYERS. THE ANNUAL NUDE RUGBY MATCH IS MORE A SPECTATOR SPORT THAN A PLAYER'S ONE, DRAWING THOUSANDS OF FANS. THE EVENT IS A DISTANT COUSIN TO A NOW-BANNED UNDIE 500, A STUDENT-RUN CAR RALLY BETWEEN CHRISTCHURCH AND DUNEDIN.

The CAPTAIN COOK TAVERN
ESTABLISHED 1860

BALDWIN ST

SCOTS IN THE SOUTH

SCOTCH WHISKEY
FINE MALT
12

THE OTAGO GOLD RUSH ERA AND LARGE-SCALE IMMIGRATION MADE DUNEDIN THE BIGGEST CITY IN NEW ZEALAND UNTIL ABOUT 1900. TODAY DUNEDIN IS STILL ONE OF THE FOUR LEADING URBAN CENTRES OF NEW ZEALAND. KNOWN FOR ITS MANY GRAND OLD BUILDINGS AND ATMOSPHERIC CHARM, DUNEDIN IS ALSO FAMOUS FOR ITS SCOTTISH CHARACTER. SCOTTISH IMMIGRANTS BROUGHT WITH THEM A ZEAL FOR EDUCATION, AS WELL AS A LOVE OF A FINE MALT WHISKEY AND THE FAMED HAGGIS CEREMONY.

BUNGY-JUMPING

BUNGY-JUMPING IS A CRAZY ADRENALIN ACTIVITY PIONEERED BY NEW ZEALANDER, AJ HACKETT. IN 1988 HE SET UP THE WORLD'S FIRST COMMERCIAL BUNGY, A 43-METRE LEAP FROM KAWARAU BRIDGE IN QUEENSTOWN. ITS HUGE POPULARITY LED TO SITES ALL OVER THE COUNTRY, WITH JUMPS AS BIG AS 134 METRES. THERE IS NEVER A SHORTAGE OF PEOPLE MAD ENOUGH TO HURL THEMSELVES FROM A GREAT HEIGHT SUPPORTED ONLY BY AN ELASTIC STRAP.

133

IT'S A MOMENT FOR ECCENTRICS TO SAVOUR - CITY SLICKERS SNOWBOARD MAIN ROADS FARMERS FORGO MILKING TO TOW TOBOGGANS BEHIND THEIR TRACTORS AND THE HARD-CORE DISPLAY UTTER INDIFFERENCE BY WEARING SHORTS AND SKIMPY DRESSES.

THIS PLUMP SHELLFISH, SAID TO BE THE WORLD'S BEST-TASTING OYSTER, HAS PUT BLUFF ON THE MAP. EVERY YEAR THE BLUFF OYSTER FLEET DREDGES THE BEDS OF ICY FOVEAUX STRAIT harvesting AROUND 9 MILLION OF THE annual 15 MILLION OYSTER QUOTA. THE COMMERCIAL VALUE OF THE CATCH CAN EXCEED $20 MILLION.

Cooking Instruction - BEST EATEN RAW, STRAIGHT FROM THE SHELL.

STEWART ISLAND

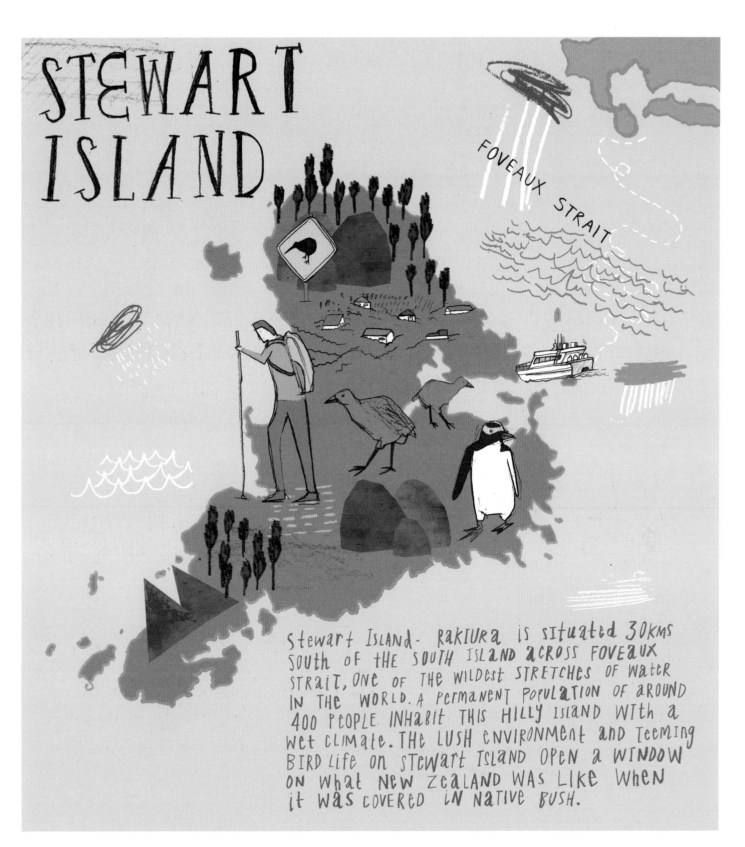

FOVEAUX STRAIT

Stewart Island- Rakiura is situated 30kms south of the South Island across Foveaux Strait, one of the wildest stretches of water in the world. A permanent population of around 400 people inhabit this hilly island with a wet climate. The lush environment and teeming bird life on Stewart Island open a window on what New Zealand was like when it was covered in native bush.

PLACES CLOSE TO OUR HEART.

MT EVEREST

ON 29 MAY, 1953 NEW ZEALAND ADVENTURER, SIR EDMUND HILLARY, AND SHERPA TENSING NORGAY, WERE THE FIRST TO CLIMB 29,035 ft TO THE TOP OF THE WORLD'S HIGHEST MOUNTAIN.

MT EREBUS

NEW ZEALAND'S DARKEST DAY - ON 28 NOVEMBER 1979, 237 PASSENGERS AND 20 CREW WERE KILLED WHEN AIR NEW ZEALAND FLIGHT TE901 CRASHED INTO THE SIDE OF MT EREBUS, ANTARCTICA.

GALLIPOLI

A DISASTROUS 9-MONTH CAMPAIGN IN 1915 FOR CONTROL OF THE GALLIPOLI PENINSULA COST 2,721 NEW ZEALANDERS THEIR LIVES - ROUGHLY ONE-QUARTER OF THOSE WHO FOUGHT AT GALLIPOLI. THE DEFEAT WAS A DEFINING MOMENT IN THE EMERGENCE OF NEW ZEALAND'S IDENTITY.

MT EVEREST

1915
ANZAC

1OZK-NZP

MT EREBUS

FLIGHT 901

GALLIPOLI

Meet the Team

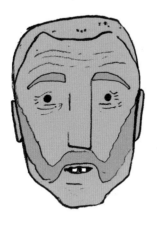 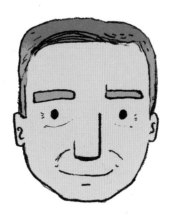  

NIGEL BECKFORD AND MICHAEL FITZSIMONS

… are professional writers and run a communications and design firm FitzBeck Creative. They've collaborated on numerous books and writing projects including, *With A Passion: The Extraordinary Passions of Ordinary New Zealanders, You Don't Take A Leap Without A Gulp: Finding the Courage to Change Careers, Navigators: Pacific Health Leaders Tell Their Stories* and *The Wellington Book.* Their business writing has been recognised with a Gold Quill Award from the International Association of Business Communicators. They received a Best Award from the Designers Institute of NZ in 2011 in the editorial and books section for their writing and art direction on *The Wellington Book.*

JESS LUNNON AND SANDI MACKECHNIE

… are illustrators/designers and recently graduated from Massey University. They have spent most waking hours for the past eighteen months researching, drawing, scanning, colouring and assembling all the elements you see in this book using a wide variety of media. Before that they worked on *The Wellington Book* for which they earned a Best Design award for their illustration/design. They have also independently each been awarded Best Design awards for their student works.